Thomas Edison

Thomas Edison's Inventions, Incredible Life, and Story of How He Changed the World

Table of Contents

Introduction

Thank you for taking the time to pick up this book all about Thomas Edison!

This book covers the topic of Thomas Edison and will teach you all about his life and incredible inventions!

As you will soon realize, Thomas Edison was an incredible pioneer, with an amazing number of inventions to his name! He has literally changed the way that we live today.

In his lifetime, Thomas Edison received over 1000 patents for his many inventions. Without his determination, focus, genius-like ability, and incredible tenacity to never give up, it is likely that the world would be now be a very different place.

This book will explain to you some of the greatest lessons that you can learn from his incredible life, to help enhance your own experience and level of success! You will learn from stories of his childhood, up-bringing, personal life, and phenomenal career.

Once again, thanks for taking the time to read this book, I hope you find it to be helpful!

Chapter 1:
The Man Behind the Name

Inventor, genius, business man, household name. These are probably all things you think about when you think Thomas Edison. However, there was much more to him than that. He was a family man as well. Later on in this book we will cover the topic of his marriages and his children.

He was a very driven man, and a very hard worker. Sometimes too hard of a worker. He would get excited about something, and tended to dive right in. He often times did not stop to think about the best way to do things, and expended a lot more effort than necessary, but he still, inevitably, got the job done.

He was very passionate about the things that he did. He would not accept anything less than perfect. Often times he would revise an idea so many times that it was unrecognizable from the beginning plan. This was the kind of man he was. He tried over and over to achieve perfection in everything that he did.

When you think of Edison, you probably think of the light bulb, but the man was so much more than just that one invention. He was also the father of recordable and playable music, among many other creations! He invented so many useful things that we still use a form of today. He was the instrument in technology.

He held many patents throughout the world, and was very well known in many countries. A very affluent man, he was well-respected by many. However, he did have a major flaw. He was very stingy, and did not like to spend much more than he absolutely had to. He often underpaid his staff and over worked them.

While he was not a perfect person, there is no disputing that the man was a powerful inventor, and without him, we would not have a lot of the stuff that we have today, and our quality of life could be very different. So, without further adieu, let us begin to learn and discover more about the man who brought us light in the darkest hours, Mr. Thomas Edison.

Chapter 2:
The Early Years

On February 11, 1847, an infant came into the world in the town of Milan, Ohio. Little did the parents know that they had given birth to someone who would become a true legend. Born under the name Thomas Alva Edison, he was the youngest of seven children, and quite possibly, the brightest.

Edison was home schooled by his mother, and much of his learning came from reading. Edison was an avid reader, often reading the most boring of manuscripts to gain additional knowledge. Stuff that would put you or I to sleep, was what kept him up at night. There was no amount of information that was not worth learning to him.

Early in his childhood, Edison was struck by a variety of ailments. He got hit with scarlet fever, which he survived, and he had several inner ear infections that were often left untreated. This caused him to have substantial hearing loss that he would later in life make up wild stories to explain.

Edison's family was not rich; they were actually quite poor. So, poor that when the railroad started to bypass Milan, they had to move for work. They moved all the way to Port Huron, Michigan, and that was when Edison had to start working to help supplement the family income. He worked two jobs, selling newspapers and candies on the railroad from Port Huron to Detroit, and he also sold vegetables as well. As he worked on the railroad, he started conducting experiments in empty boxcars. Unfortunately, one of his experiments went awry, and he caught a boxcar on fire. This was when he began the rumors about his hearing loss. He attributed it to the conductor pulling him out of the train by his ears, and boxing them as he got off at the station.

After the railroad, Edison decided to go solo on his newspaper expeditions. The newspaper company he worked for agreed, as they did not want any more mishaps like the one on the train to be their responsibility. He gathered up a few friends, and together they printed their own paper to sell with the papers that they were already selling. The paper they sold, the Grand Trunk Herald, did so well that Edison began to see a future as an entrepreneur. In fact, eventually he became such a good businessman that he started up fourteen successful businesses. One of which is still a major brand today, and that you may have a product from in your home right now. The General Electric brand, or GE for short.

On one of his paper expeditions, Edison saved a three-year-old boy from being hit by a train that had derailed and was careening out of control in their direction. The father of the boy was so pleased and grateful, that he offered Edison a job on the spot. Edison agreed, and was trained to be a telegraph operator at once. He worked for a while in Port Huron, but once he was ready to go it alone, he took a telegraphing job in Ontario.

When Edison turned nineteen, he took off for Louisville. Yes, Louisville Kentucky. The farthest place away from Ontario he could have possibly gone it seems. He took a job with Western Union. One of the country's largest telegraphing companies around. He worked the night shift of the news wire, and since in those days not much went on at night, he had plenty of time for reading. With reading, came experimenting, and when an experiment went wrong, he got fired.

After he was fired in Kentucky, he moved to Elizabeth, New Jersey. Here he found a mentor that allowed Edison to live in the basement of his home until he established himself. Franklin Leonard Pope was a telegrapher and inventor like Edison, but with more knowledge. Once Edison had begun learning from Pope, he started working on his own inventions. At this point in time, his inventions mainly dealt with telegraphy, such as a stock ticker. However, his first patent was for an electric vote counter. His patent was granted shortly after he turned 21.

Shortly after he got his first patent, he opened up a few shops. They were pretty successful, and he was even able to hire a few employees. One of which was Mary Stillwell. Edison fell for her the moment he met her in his shop, and two months later, they were married. They had been married for two years, when their first child arrived. Marion Estelle Edison was their first-born child, and she was nicknamed Dot. Three years later, they had a boy. They named him Thomas Alva Edison Jr, and gave him the nickname Dash. (Seeing the telegraph theme here?) Two years after the birth of little Dash, they had another son by the name of William Leslie Edison. He had no nickname, but is the only one who is documented to have gone to college. He also followed in his father's footsteps and became an inventor.

Sadly, at age 29 and after thirteen short years of marriage, Mary died of unknown causes. Some attribute it to a possible brain tumor, but it was more likely that she died of morphine poisoning, as it was a common medicine in those days, and no one knew of the ghastly side effects. So, that left Edison to raise three pre-adolescent children on his own. However, he continued to invent, and still was a great father to his children.

He would not have to raise them alone however, as just two short years later, he married Mina Miller, the daughter of Lewis Miller, an inventor that Edison both admired and respected. They had three children together as well. A girl and two boys just like with his previous wife. The children were, Madeline Edison, and she grew up to marry John Eyre Sloan. Charles Edison, governor of New Jersey from 1941-1944, and who later took on his father's businesses when he passed, and Theodore Miller Edison, who graduated out of MIT's Physics department, and has more than eighty patents accredited to him. This time, Edison's wife outlived him, and they were married to the end of his days.

In his early days, Edison had several inventions that went unnoticed. He had many devices for improving telegraphic function, such as his automatic repeater, but no one really attributed these to his name. However, in 1877, he invented the phonograph. It was the biggest invention that he had ever created, and had more success than he had ever dreamed possible. Most people thought that it had to be magical, and called Edison the Wizard of Menlo Park. It recorded sound on tinfoil around circular grooves, and was only useful for a few plays. Nonetheless, the public was smitten with this device, and it got Edison recognized across the nation. He even got invited to the White House to showcase his invention. However, he did not expand on the phonograph further, and it was not until Alexander Graham Bell took over the idea that it was made to be any better than it was when Edison first designed it.

Edison designed a quadruplex telegraph, and sold it to Western Union. He was surprised that they offered him ten thousand dollars for the invention, and of course he graciously accepted. It gave him the funds he needed to build an industrial research lab in Menlo Park. It was his first shop that was designed to bring out constant innovation in technology. While Edison had people to do a lot of the research and development, they did only under his instruction.

Edison was known for being hard on his workers, paying them low wages and making them work extra-long hours until they had a task finished. However, his workers learned a lot, and some were able to even go and get their own patents. If a worker did a good job, they were praised, and often got a raise depending on the amount of work they did. However, the raises were often minor. Thus, Edison was portrayed as a cruel boss, and a stingy man.

Edison hired William Joseph Hammer in 1879. Hammer was instrumental in Edison's design of electric incandescent lamps. Hammer was promoted to chief engineer of Edison Lamps Works. In his first year, he produced fifty thousand lamps, and impressed Edison, earning the title, Pioneer of Incandescence Electric Lighting. Under Hammer's prompting, Edison hired Frank J. Sprague, a valued mathematician who handled the mathematical aspects of the research, as Edison was not prone to using mathematics himself. However, when his other workers brought up great mathematical values, he was known to use them in his designs to help make them better, as he was not averse to math, he just preferred not to do it himself.

Edison was known to have employed some of the greatest minds in history. It is no surprise with the fact that eventually his research lab expanded over two city blocks, and had almost every material conceivable to the human mind available. This lab was not the only one to be in existence though, as more were built later on in his life.

During Edison's early years, while many boys were out working to help bring home food for their family, Edison was becoming an inventor on top of doing multiple jobs to keep bringing in an income. There are many different accounts of him losing his jobs due to experimenting while working, but he always found another job shortly after that.

It was in these years that Edison started his own businesses, and discovered that he was a great business man, and was very savvy. That is a feat for most young men. They are just beginning to learn what trade they are good in, and still have years to go before they open their own shops, but Edison opened several at an early age. That is due in part to him not having to do a long apprenticeship, as electricity was still a fairly new concept, and people who knew how to work with it were few and far between. This left a good open market for those who wished to get patents, and start a business up in the field, without having to have a signature of a master.

Chapter 3:
The Inventions and Companies
of Edison

There are many things that the man invented. And we still use a lot of them today. Some of the inventions, you may not even realize that he created, but they were in fact, his inventions. Here are some of the key inventions of Thomas Edison, along with some of the different companies he started.

Phonograph: This is the oldest version of the record player. It had a large horn on the end that was used as a speaker, and it had to be cranked up to play. The disks it used were circular pieces of tin foil that had sound lines etched into them. A needle dug along the grooves, and made the sound come out of the giant horn like speaker in music form. Many people felt that this invention was magical, because there had never been anything like it seen before. It was the greatest invention of the time. However, Alexander Graham Bell often gets credit for the phonograph because Edison did not try to better the invention so when the protection limit hit on the patent, Graham Bell took it over, and made it better.

When was the last time you listened to music? Today? Yesterday? Chances are, you don't go very long without listening to music. Imagine if the technology wasn't there to listen to the bands that you love, and you would have to go without the songs they sing for long periods of time until you could see them play in person. Well even then, it would be different. They would be using all acoustic equipment, and not many people could attend because there would be no voice amplification. The phonograph was a big stride in recording and playing sound, and if Edison had not come up with the idea, then we may not have the musical devices that we have today!

Electrical Lighting: This is the category that Edison is seemingly most known for. While he was not the first person to try to create incandescent lighting, he was the first to come up with the design of the light bulb as we know it today. He tried many different ideas but was having a lot of trouble making the bulb's light be long lasting. He knew that he had to get high resistance so that the bulb would not need a lot of electricity to emit light, and when he achieved that, he had a hard time finding a filament that could hold up to that amount of resistance. However, inspiration hit when he and a few members of his team took a vacation to Wyoming to visit Battle Lakes, and watch the total solar eclipse that year. Edison started examining the bamboo on his fishing rod, and that gave him the idea to use a bamboo filament, which would burn for up to twelve hundred hours. Edison hoped that he could rival the lighting of gas and kerosene lamps. Little did he know that he would completely wipe out the need for them in just a few short years.

Edison did a demonstration of his light bulb, and a railroad owner that attended wanted Edison to install his lights on the new steamer they were building. Edison agreed, and the Columbia was installed with the first commercial use of the electric lamp created by Edison Electric Light Company.

However, it was not all roses with Edison, as he had many people try to sue him, saying that he used their design, and he had many competitors trying to create what he did for a lot cheaper. Such as induction lighting, which his rival, George Westinghouse bought the patent for. It was cheaper that incandescent lighting, but much more dangerous, and was known to cause fires. However, people were taking the risk to save money. This forced Edison to lower his prices, and make his product more affordable on the market.

Electric lamps and light bulbs have become a necessity in our generation. Electricity in general is a necessity today. If we don't have it, we panic. Our food spoils. We can't get a hold of anyone after a few hours, because our phones die. Electricity has become such an important part of our everyday lives, and it is partially because Edison made that first stride and did not give up on the idea of incandescent lighting.

Electric Power Distribution: Edison wanted to make electricity as easy to obtain as gas, and so he created a company that distributed electric power much like the gas utilities were distributed. He used the first steam powered electricity distributor, and it used DC current. While electricity was still not widespread house to house, this made it a lot easier for the general public to obtain electricity.

However, he had a lot of rivalries with Tesla designing AC power. The alternating currents allowed electricity to travel over hundreds of miles, and reach people even in the rural areas. Tesla sold his patent to Westinghouse, and AC won the game. However, the alternating currents are often too dangerous for certain appliances, so the DC adapter must be used. Such as the brick on your laptop chord.

Fluoroscopy: Edison designed the first ever commercial use fluoroscope. This used x-rays to make an image on a radiograph plate. These calcium tungstate plates were a lot better than the platinocyanide plates that had previously been used, as the fluoroscope plates produced a much better picture. In fact, they are still used today. However, working around radiation for so long almost cost Edison his eyesight, and killed his assistant who volunteered to be a test subject for

Edison. By 1903, he was so afraid of x-ray machines that he even refused to talk about them.

Have you ever broken a bone? Or thought that you had broken one? If you have at some point in your life, you most likely had an x-ray done of the afflicted area. The plate that they attach the magnet on is a flouroscope plate. It is the same type of plate that Edison used to show the x-rays back in the old days, however, now it can be transmitted to the computer, rather than have to stay on the plate. This saves a lot of money because calcium tungstate can get rather expensive. The concept remains the same however, and thus Edison's work is still used today in hospitals.

Telegraph Improvements: Edison began in the telegraphy business, and so it makes sense that some of his first patents were in telegraphy. He made the stock ticker, which was the first telegraph broadcaster that was completely electric based. He also made the first two-way telegraph, and a quadruplex telegraph. These allowed him to get into the world of inventing, and even make some money to fund his other inventions. The quadruplex telegraph made him the money he needed to build his lab in Menlo park.

The telegraph was the first way of communication across long distances and it was very important. Especially during the war. The telegraphs were sent in Morse code, and you had to add a stop after every word. However, during the war, sometimes telegraphs would be sent without any stops to confuse the enemy if it fell into the wrong hands. Or the stops would be put in random places. The telegraph was basically an extremely old and very limited email.

Motion Picture Camera: Edison created the very first motion picture camera and the very first motion picture viewer. The camera, or kineograph was created by WKL Dickinson and Edison together. Edison worked on the energy and mechanics of the camera, and Dickinson, a photographer, worked on the optics of the camera. The kinetoscope was used to view the short films made by the kineograph.

A bigger version of the kinetoscope, the vitoscope, was used to project these films onto larger screens. An old-style projector, if you will. The vitascope was very popular in New York City, and Edison designed cylinders that you could add voice overs for the films on, and manually synchronize it with the movie.

However, despite the vitascope being good for a bigger audience, the kinetoscope was the most popular of the two, as it was more suitable for a private setting. It was sold all over the world, and made a fortune. Edison made many short films of many different types. In fact, the first Frankenstein was filmed with a kineograph and shown on the kinetoscopes.

Today, we have high definition televisions and can take videos with our cell phones. Movies come equipped with soundtracks and speaking already recorded on them. These advances would not have even been possible had Edison not acted upon the thought of making the kineograph, and had just left the thought in the back of his mind.

Those are only some of the inventions that Edison created, but they are some of the most important to our history. He had several minor inventions as well. The man had well over a thousand patents to his name, and very few were ever disputed as being someone else's work.

Edison was also a very savvy business man. He owned and operated many businesses, and had a hand in a lot more than he owned. There are also some countries that used his name to exploit his genius, and those will be noted here as well. Here are the companies that Edison was involved in or owned.

Lansden Company: This was an automobile company that Edison owned a good portion of in controlling interest. Eventually he tired of the automobile industry and sold his interest, and moved on to other companies.

Battery Supplies Company: Former Edison employees started up this company to sell batteries and their accessories. However, they had stolen the ideas from Edison, and he sued them for patent infringement. After a long litigation process, a settlement was reached, and Edison purchased the company, making it his own, and then legally dissolved it three years later.

Deustche Edison Accumulatoren Company: This was an exploitation company in Berlin. It was backed by the bank, and really had nothing to do with Edison, other than covertly using his name to sell storage batteries.

Edison Gelleschaft: A legal German branch of an Edison company. It sold a lot of his inventions such as the phonograph and kinetoscopes. It was managed by Thomas Graf for years. It even ran for a while during the war, and kept a small office even after the big company itself absolved. The office continued running until the retirement of Graf.

Edison Manufacturing Company: Edison's personal company. Originally started up to sell primary batteries, it began selling Edison's other inventions as well pretty soon after the beginning. It started in New Jersey, and expanded across the country. Eventually, it became to Thomas A. Edison Inc, and was dissolved shortly thereafter.

Other Battery Companies: We could go on all day about the many battery companies that Edison was a part of. He would start a company only to dissolve it a few years later when he thought of a better idea. He was not very fond of just fixing what he had, he had to start brand new every time. He had many other minor battery companies that often didn't last more than a year before they were dissolved, and a new one was created.

Cement Companies: Edison was very big in the Cement company business. He had about five cement company businesses, and they distributed everything from cement itself to architecture and tools to handle the cement. The biggest one of these was the Edison Portland Cement Company. It produced cement all across the US and Canada. It had mills in many places, and while it started in 1899, it did not dissolve until 1931. One of the longest lasting cement companies he ever started.

Edison General Electric: Edison created a general electric company to get electricity to the people. Eventually he merged with Thomson-Houston and dropped his name from the title, and it was called General Electric company. General Electric is still in use today, providing everything from light bulbs to household appliances. Today it has been shortened to GE for General Electric.

Commonwealth Edison: A fuel company that Edison invested in, and is now known as Exelon.

As you can see, Edison had quite the range of companies. Cement, mining, electric, batteries, telegraphy, and much, much more. He was a very important investor in many small companies, as well as starting up his own. He started the film industry, and he started the cement business. While he did not succeed in mining, he used his ideas in the field elsewhere in life.

Chapter 4:
Edison and Tesla

It is no secret that Thomas Edison and Nikola Tesla were not the best of friends. Throughout their lives, they were feuding, trying to be the best inventor in the world of electricity. Tesla would often make outrageous claims, such as being able to build a palm sized earthquake machine. He made these claims to try to make himself seem better than Edison, as often times Edison out performed him in new inventions.

What may have not been widely known is that Tesla once worked for Edison. He was an employee in the Menlo Park research lab for quite a while before he and Edison butted heads. Tesla wanted to improve the efficiency on many of Edison's prototypes. Edison jokingly said that if Tesla could he would award him fifty thousand dollars. When Tesla did, Edison explained that it was an American style joke, and he was not really giving up fifty thousand dollars for something that might have saved him two thousand dollars' total. Edison, a virtuous man, offered Tesla a whopping ten dollars a week raise however. Tesla was too prideful to take the raise, though, and quit. He then spent several years doing odd jobs just to get by.

Eventually, Tesla made enough money to start up his own company, and then the rivalry began. Tesla started the concept of alternating current in electricity, which while it took more energy to produce, was better for transmitting a lot of power over long distances. Edison went for a direct current, which took less energy to produce, but was not practical for large volumes of electricity.

Tesla patented many different inventions, but he wasn't just out to beat Edison, he wanted to hit him where it hurt the most. So, he went to Edison's rival, George Westinghouse and sold him his patents. Westinghouse had the money, and Tesla had the ideas, and when AC power won out, it left a really bitter taste in Edison's mouth.

Imagine how much power we would have today if the two had just worked together the entire time. We would possibly be steps ahead of where we are today, and probably lest wasteful with our energy, because instead of feuding and having to use transformers for AC/DC currents, they would likely have found a way to make them work together to reduce energy waste, and bring the most efficiency into the mix.

The two men were very different, yet strikingly alike. While Tesla was a germaphobe, and Edison was not very hygienic, the two men were both egocentric geniuses, who could not stand egocentricity in others. They were both very proud, and very sure of themselves. They were both outstanding inventors who had more of a grasp of how to work with electricity than any inventor we see today.

Chapter 5:
Stories from Edison's Life

There are many stories from Edison's life. Whether they are true or not, it is unclear, but they are enjoyable nonetheless. Edison's life is surrounded by mysteries and stories. Some people believed that the man was sent from the future to bring knowledge of electricity to the people around him. Others thought he was a wizard. He was even thought by some to be an alien. He was so innovative with his inventions for the time; it was thought to be unreal. In fact, as stated above, people could not wrap their heads around the fact that the phonograph was not a magical piece of equipment, and was in fact, a real invention.

Edison himself was a mystery, and liked to perpetuate stories. He felt that it added to his reputation, and made him seem more of a god in the engineering front. He loved being revered, and would often times add to the tales to make himself seem that much greater, and make his products that much more desirable.

Here are two fantastic stories from his life, starting in his early childhood.

1. "Addled"

A young boy by the name of Thomas Edison came home from school one day, and in his hand, he carried a note from his teacher. He skipped through the front door, not knowing what was in the note in his hand, for he could not yet read.

"Mamma. I got a note from school today!" He shouted as he ran through the door.

"Oh really, son? Let me see it." She replied, wondering what possibly the teacher could need to write home about.

However, she soon understood, as she read the note in her head. The note read:

Dear Mrs. Edison

I am writing to inform you that your son, Thomas, is addled, and we would no longer like for him to return to school. We cannot handle him.

Sincerely,

His Teacher

Thomas Edison's mother burst into tears, as she could not believe what she was reading. She felt that her son was very bright, and was not, in fact, mentally ill.

"What's wrong Mamma, did I do something bad?" Thomas asked, upon seeing his mother's tears.

"No son. These are tears of joy." She lied quickly. She never wanted her son to know the truth. So, she read the note aloud but changed the reason for why he was not to return to school

"Dear Mrs. Edison: Your son, Thomas is a genius, and we cannot teach him anymore. Please teach him yourself. Sincerely, His teacher."

"Really, Mamma? I am a genius?" Thomas asked, astounded.

"Yes, son, you are."

From that moment on, his mother taught him at home. She taught him how to read, despite his dyslexia, and she taught him how to do math, and all about science. She taught him a love for the arts, and gave him a thirst for knowledge. Eventually, Thomas grew to be a genius, as his mother had once believed he could be. He became enamored with learning, and wanted to know everything that he could. Though his family was not rich, he managed to get plenty of reading material, by finding what people had thrown out, such as periodicals, and newspapers. He talked to other people a lot, and learned from them as well. He was never satisfied with what he knew, rather, he wanted to learn more.

When Thomas was thirteen, his mother passed away. As he was going through her things, he found the letter that his teacher had wrote, back when he was a little boy. He read the truth for the first time. That he was believed to be mentally ill, and was not welcomed back at school. He wrote in his diary later that night

Thomas Edison was an addled boy, who thanks to a hero mother, became a genius.

Edison never forgot the amount of love his mother gave him that day, by deciding not to listen to the words of a teacher, but rather her own heart, and put in time and effort to unlock the genius hidden inside of him.

Edison was not the best in school when he was a little boy. He had a hard time reading, and a hard time focusing. He could not stay on one task at a time, and for this, his teachers believed that he was mentally ill. However, they failed to realize that he was a genius in the making, something his mother did not overlook.

2. Morse code marriage

Edison was known to have two marriages. The first was to Mary Stilwell, whom he married two months after meeting, and she was an employee at one of his shops. However, shortly after marrying her, he found that she was not able to invent, and was often exasperated by hearing of his many inventions, as she believed there was a world outside of inventing. However, he remained married to her for thirteen years until the day she died, and they had three children together.

Then Edison's world changed, when he befriended a couple by the surname of Gilliard. The Gilliard's made it their mission to set Edison up with a suitable young lady, which was not as simple as you might think. Edison was not the best-looking guy in the world, as he was slightly bug eyed, and had really bad dandruff. To top it all off, he was hard of hearing, so he had to lean very close to the ladies' faces to hear them. This often caused them extreme discomfort, and Edison was not too keen on them as well, as they had typical interests, and were not into inventing.

That was, until the Gilliard's invited Mina Miller over when Edison was visiting. Mina was not put off by Edison's need to be really close to hear, nor was she disturbed by his looks. She was enthralled by his talk of inventions, as she was the daughter of an inventor herself. When Edison went back to the city, he found himself so smitten with Mina that he could not focus on his work. His journal was full of entries about how much he thought of her, and how he knew that he had to see her again.

He went back to the Gilliard's, and they again invited Mina over, as she was as excited to see him again, and he was her. They talked some more, and eventually, they started communicating more and more outside of the Gilliard establishment. He taught her Morse code so that they would be able to talk in private even in the company of others. They would be at her family's house, and would talk about things completely different than what her parents were talking about, and no one was any the wiser, as it was done by tapping on each other's hands. One day, Edison tapped out on Mina's hand. -- --- ..- .-.. -.. -.-- --- ..- -- .- .-. .-. -.-- -- . (Will you marry me?) to which Mina replied -.-- . ... (Yes). So they were wed not long after, and that is the story of how Thomas Edison proposed using Morse code.

Chapter 6:
Things You Can Learn from Edison

There are many things that you can learn from Edison's life and how he lived. The man was a walking inspiration if you only knew where to look. There are many things that you can learn from his life, and things you can learn from his inventions. This chapter is all about what you can learn from his life, and how you can apply it to your own.

This is what Edison did while he lived with his mentor for a while. He studied the man that he looked up to, and he learned about things that he could use to better himself. Things from the man's past that he had overcome, to inspire Edison whenever he got discouraged. Ideas that the man was stumped on, Edison took and made better. Edison was constantly learning things to improve his existence.

So, what can you learn from him? Read below to find out.

<u>Learn</u>

It is never too late to learn something new. Edison was constantly learning new things, even as he got older. From the time, he was a young boy to the time he died, he never lost his voracity for learning. If there was something new to read, he read it. If there was a new demonstration, he went to it. If one of his workers had learned something new, he wanted to know about it as well. He was never satisfied with what he knew.

That is how you can learn from him. In today's age, a lot of people go to school, and listen to what they are taught, and take it at that. No one ever questions what they have learned, or tries to go out and learn more on a subject that there was not much information on. There is only so much time that you are in school, yet there is so much to learn. You cannot possibly learn it all in those twelve short years that you spend in the four prison like walls. Besides, school is supposed to teach you how to learn, if you don't use those skills outside of the classroom, what are you even showing up for?

Challenge what you learn as well. Is it completely factually accurate, or is it a glossy representation because they feel the truth is too gruesome for you? Go to the library and check out a book on the subject you are challenging. In fact, check out several books on the subject. Make sure that some of them are biographies from the people that actually experienced it. Read them. Be like Edison, never be satisfied until you have read everything you possibly could about the subject you're interested in.

Don't just learn from books, though. Learn from other people. Ask questions, hear their story. Walk down your street. If you live in a more populated area, chances are you have seen a homeless person on the streets. Talk to one, or talk to many. They are people and they have stories. If you think that they are criminals, or otherwise have an aversion to them, you will be surprised to learn about the circumstances that got them there in the first place. A lot of them are disabled veterans. Once you have learned about the hardships in life, and learned about the people who would love what we all take for granted, you can move on to other people. A musician, or an artist. Someone in a line of work that you are interested in. Talk, ask questions, and truly listen to the answers you get. This is what Edison did. He learned from others almost as much as he learned from books. Be like Edison and never stop learning.

You can also learn from the workplace as well. Even if you are in a job where you think you could learn nothing. A lot of people view fast food jobs this way, however that is the farthest from the truth. You can learn a lot from even the smallest of jobs. You can learn everything from how to leave your problems at the door, to real and valuable people skills.

How you can apply this to your life

Everything you learn, you can carry with you. You would be surprised when you might need to know something about an obscure subject. Remembering things that might seem irrelevant can help you in your future, because if you are ever in a tight situation, you can use your knowledge to help you figure out a solution. This is what Edison did. He learned about everything he could, and used it in his experiments. A good motto to use is: When in doubt, learn it.

<u>Persevere</u>

 Edison was the type of person who never gave up. If he couldn't figure something out, he would try until he finally got it right. He would try a million and one ways, and if those did not work, he would try a million and one more. Sure, he got frustrated, but he kept going. He would spend long hours in his lab working, and he often did not sleep for more than a few hours a night until he got everything just right. His mind was constantly working, and eventually he would get the right result.

In today's age, too many people give up if they can't achieve something right away. They try a new hobby, and think that if they don't reach expert levels on the first try that they are not good enough, and they just give up. This is the opposite of what you should do. Rome was not built in a day, and neither is a new skill. You have to keep trying until you reach the desirable end result. Edison was a perfect embodiment of "practice makes perfect" and "if at first you don't succeed, try, try again". This was because he never gave up, and you shouldn't either.

Say, for example, you are trying to cook a new dish. You get all of the ingredients together, and you put it in, and you cook it. You follow the directions to a 't' and still it doesn't come out tasting quite right. Do you throw in the towel, and say you are never making that dish again? No. You try it a different way. Sure, the directions may say one thing, but sometimes you have to try things that may not seem obvious. Try adding a different seasoning, or cooking it for a little less time or a little more time. Make more mistakes, and learn what not to do. Eventually that dish will be a favorite of the household. Keep trying, because that is the only way that you will succeed.

For example, crocheting can be tough for beginners. This is a hard skill to learn, and it takes a lot of patience and perseverance to get it right. You will not be able to whip up a pair of socks in two hours on your first try. First you have to be proficient at making a simple pot holder or scarf, and go from there. If you make a mistake, don't throw in the towel, try again. Keep trying until you have become good enough to make the thing that you want to make, and when you get good enough at that, you can try something else, and it will get a lot easier to try higher level things. This applies to almost every endeavor in life.

How you can apply this to your life

Like the above examples state, you can use these to succeed at new hobbies or even a new job. You just have to keep trying when you make a mistake. Remember, you do not fail, you merely find ways to do it wrong. That is a mantra that you should remember, as it is actually quite inspiring when you think about it. You made a mistake, so what, that is one more way not to do it, so keep going until you find the way to do it right.

Take risks

This is one of the most important things that Edison did. He caught fire on a box car due to one of these risks. Yet he kept on going with his risks and his experiments. Edison never let a little danger, or discomfort stop him, and though there were some consequences, he kept on going, taking even more risks. Whether they were physically or financially, he took them.

A lot of people are scared to take risks, and they stay in the same rut that they are in, and complain that life is boring. Some people take risks such as bungee jumping or skydiving, and they seem a lot happier, but thrill risks are not the only risks in life. Going for that big job you always wanted, even if it means moving to an entirely new area, asking a crush out on a date, buying a new car. All of these are risks that you could take, and they could potentially bring so much more joy to life if you did take them.

Think of something risky you would never do. Now think of the success you could have if you did take that risk and it paid off. Money, fame, happiness? The riskiest things are generally the most rewarding. If you are not willing to quit your job to try to get the bigger one, maybe try just applying to the bigger one first, and keep your job that you are currently in. Just applying is a risk in itself, because you are putting yourself out there and getting your hopes up, and you might not get the job, which could be devastating. You have to take the risk with the feeling that it is going to pay off.

You can also take a risk by investing money into a company to buy controlling interest. This is something that Edison did quite frequently. He would invest in a company, whether the company was destined to succeed or fail. If he liked the concept, he put his money on the line. Most of the time, with Edison's help, the company succeeded until he decided to sell off his stocks in the company, then they would either fail shortly thereafter, or continue succeeding. Invest in something that is just starting up. Even if it is a small amount at first. The more you put yourself out there, the more reward you stand to receive. That makes life more enjoyable, even if you don't get the gold, you still participated in the race, and that is what is fun in life. Trying new things and taking risks.

How you can apply this to your life

You don't have to jump off of tall buildings, or out of an airplane unless that is what you are into, but taking risks can fulfill areas in your life that you feel are lacking something. This makes life more colorful, and more enjoyable. Imagine what it would be like if you could wake up each day and look forward to the day ahead, even on Mondays. It is a nice thought, and it is possible if you start taking risks. Sure, playing it safe keeps you from getting hurt, but half of the fun in life is the thrill of doing something that is not the safest thing to be doing. The thrill of failure, or the thrill of the risk of failure to be more precise.

Keep Moving

 This is one thing that Edison did quite well. Whenever he invented something, and got it to where it was the best that he thought he could get it to, he moved on to something else. He did not spend his whole life on one invention, which is why he had over a thousand patents in his lifetime. He constantly kept moving on to new things, and tried to create as many things as he could, and would often have several projects going at once. While he did not give up until the invention was complete, he did not devote his life to that single invention until it was done, rather he would go work on something else, and often get an idea from another invention.

Today's society is so caught up in the idea that you have to finish something before you can move on. Reading books for instance, most people look down on those who read multiple books at one time and say that they person has an issue with commitment, when in reality for them it may be difficult to stay focused on one thing at a time. That is how it often was for Edison. The best things in life come in pairs they always say, so why do we have to focus on only one thing at a time? If you are doing a job, you have to focus on the job you are doing. You are not allowed to be at work and check your stock market values at the same time. You have to wait until your workday is over, or until you get a break. If you are working on a project, you have to finish that project before you can move on to the next one. Especially in school. If you are doing a project for one lesson and you know what the project is going to be for the next lesson, you still have to finish the one you are on before going to the next thing. You can't finish both and turn them in at the same time, because you will get reprimanded for not focusing enough on the task at hand.

This is a very limiting type of instruction. The mind is designed to multitask, and handle multiple things at one time, and by training your mind to only handle one thing at a time, you are doing yourself a disservice, because there are times where you are going to have to do a few things at one time, and if you have trained your brain away from that, you will get overwhelmed. You have to keep your mind ready to multitask, and to be able to take on multiple things at once.

You have to multitask to work in fast food for example, and if you are used to focusing on one task at a time, it can be exceedingly difficult, because often times you have to take an order while serving someone else, and make sure that food is not burning. You have to learn to focus on multiple things at the same time, rather than give things your undivided attention. This is something that Edison learned at an early age. He would often work on experiments while working at a job. Sometimes it caused problems, but that is the risk he was willing to take to become a great inventor.

How you can apply this to your life

Retrain your brain. You have to be able to multitask to become the person you want to be. Most high-level jobs, you generally only have to focus on one thing, but in lower level jobs, you have to focus on many. That is a problem with society though. They train you for the higher-level jobs, not the lower level ones that you have to start at to make it to the top. So, you have to retrain your mind yourself, and make sure that you have sufficiently learned how to multitask.

You can also take this with you when you are learning new skills. You can learn multiple new skills at one time, rather than learning one and moving on to another, and so on and so forth. This saves time, as you can use things that you are learning in one skill to help you learn more in another skill. This was Edison's way of thinking. Doing something on one invention could help him solve a problem on another invention. It can help you as well.

Encourage Others

 Edison's mother encouraged him to be the best he could be, even though she had been told that he was addled. She worked really hard, because she believed that in her son was a genius just waiting to be released. As told in the story in the previous chapter, she did not tell Edison that he was mentally ill, and so he never knew. He believed that he could do anything.

In the same style, we should treat others well. Rather than dragging them down, we should help them to believe that they are capable of doing whatever they set their minds too, regardless of disability. Just as we should encourage ourselves.

This world can be so full of negativity. If someone comes home with a note from school saying their child is not fit for a normal classroom, and instead needs special education because the teachers can't handle them, the parents often don't pull the child out and homeschool them themselves. Rather they let their child feel like they are not good enough to succeed, and plant that seed of doubt in their child's mind. If they see someone who is trying to do what they believe can't be done, they say that it is impossible and that the person should just give up. We also tear ourselves down. Whenever we think of doing something that is hard, our brains kick in to say that it is impossible, and it shouldn't even be attempted. We are our own self destroyers, and we are very good at bringing ourselves down. This causes us to bring others down as well.

We need to get away from that trend, and back to encouraging people to be the best they can be. Edison didn't invent the light bulb by saying that it is impossible, he invented it because people believed in him, and he believed that it could be done. We have to build ourselves, and others up. If you see someone attempting something hard, encourage them, and see if there is anything you can do to help them achieve their goal, rather than telling them it can't be done. That is not caring. A good friend or family member does everything in their power to help that person succeed, not tell them to not even try so they don't fail.

How you can apply this to your life

Encourage others. You never know when you might be the reason they succeed. You never know how much confidence you gave them, or how close they could have been to giving up. Encourage yourself on something that you feel may be hard to do, rather than discouraging yourself to save yourself from failure, for not trying is the surest way to fail.

As you can see, there are several things that you can learn from Edison, and how he lived his life. The man was constantly learning, and in that fashion, you should strive to do the same. The more you know, the more you can grow. The more knowledge you receive, the farther you can take yourself. And who knows, if you learn some things from other humans, you might find some new friends. People are very interesting and there is much to learn from them. There is also much to learn from books as well, as books have a history just waiting to be unleashed. If you go to your library, there are millions of pages of knowledge sitting patiently, waiting to be read, and learned from. You can learn so much from the world, so get out and explore it.

You also can learn about taking risks from him. Not settling for the same old same old every day. Taking risks can bring a joy to your life that you probably didn't even realize was possible. You can also learn from taking a risk. You can learn what works for you and what does not work for you so that you can have that knowledge for when you try again and take the risk once more.

This leads us to perseverance. Edison was a firm believer in never giving up. He tried a million and one ways on every invention he ever created. He would work long hours, and produce brilliant results, but just because he was a genius does not mean that he didn't have his struggles. The fluoroscope was one of those problems that he had. He had a hard time getting it quite right, and he suffered because of it, but he never gave up.

Encourage others to persevere as well, as Edison's mother did for him. The world is so full of other people trying to bring each other down, it doesn't need any more. Be the one to build them up. Build yourself up as well. You never succeed when you don't even try. Be the one to push yourself to success.

And last but not least, Edison did not focus on anything for too long. He often jumped from task to task, starting one, and then another and jumping between them as he saw fit. If he got stumped on one, he would move to another, and hoped that he could learn something from the new task to put towards the other task he was stuck on. It is in the same fashion that we should try to take on multiple tasks rather than getting stuck on one, and not being able to move forward until it is done, creating a halt in productivity. Instead we should have multiple tasks running, so that we can always be working on something, and always moving forward!

Chapter 7:
The Light Bulb

Of course, a book on Thomas Edison would not be complete without properly documenting his most famous invention – the light bulb.

What you may not know is, Edison was not the original inventor of the light bulb. He was however, the one who invented the first commercially viable one.

The first light bulb is actually believed to have been invented back in 1802! In fact, Edison is only one of 24 people who are believed to have experimented with light bulbs before Edison's commercial design was released!

Why is Edison Credited with Inventing the Light Bulb?

So, if all of these other inventors and scientists were already working with light bulbs, why is it that Edison is so commonly referred to as having invented them?

Well, as previously mentioned, it is primarily due to the fact that he designed and created the first commercially viable type. Prior to Edison's design, light bulbs were inefficient and did not last a long time. Overall, they were inferior to gas lamps, and were not used to illuminate people's homes.

Edison saw the potential however, and set about making the perfect design!

The Design Process

Edison's work on the light bulb first began in 1878, some 76 years after the original one was produced! Later in the year, he filled his first light-related patent.

The light bulb was possibly one of Edison's most testing inventions. During the design process he ran into a lot of problems, and tested using a multitude of different materials.

Initially, his designs used a range of different metal filaments, including platinum. Platinum was not an ideal material however, as it was expensive, difficult to work with, and would require large copper conductors to be powered properly.

Later, Edison experimented with carbon-based filaments. After one year, Edison had created a prototype with a carbon based filament that managed to stay alight for 13.5 hours – a new record!

The filaments he used were carbon-cardboard filaments, that burned well compared to previous designs, but were not really suitable for commercial application.

The breakthrough came however, several months later when Edison and his team discovered carbon-bamboo filaments. These new filaments managed to burn for an incredible 1200 hours!

Just one year later, Edison began created commercial bamboo lamps.

The perfectionist he was; Edison was never satisfied. Throughout his career he continued to work on his light bulb design. He constantly strived to make it better, safer, and more efficient.

Soon, electric lamps became cheap and readily available to the mass-market, changing the way people illuminate their homes worldwide!

Chapter 8:
Elephant Execution

In 1903, Edison tested a different use of electricity – execution.

During the time, elephants were often used as attractions in America, and were grossly mistreated. The elephants would often become violent, injuring or killing people. When this occurred, the elephant would be put to death, usually by hanging.

At Luna Park in Coney Island, there was an elephant named Topsy. Topsy was primarily used as an attraction, but was also put to work carrying heavy building materials. During her short time at Luna Park, Topsy managed to injure several people, and even kill a spectator.

During this time period, Edison was directly competing with Nikola Tesla. Edison was pushing for his DC current method to be the main form of power used, whereas Tesla was a proponent of AC.

Edison was trying to prove the dangers of Tesla's AC method, and regularly used it to put down stray and unwanted animals.

Once Topsy's death sentence came, the owner's suggested the usual method of hanging. The ASPCA president of the time, John Haynes, said no to the proposed hanging due to it being too inhumane.

This was where Edison came in. Together with the owners of Luna Park, they decided upon a public execution of Topsy, which was approved by Haynes.

The execution was a public event, and many people attended the spectacle. The Luna Park owner's initially planned to charge a 25cent admission fee, but they didn't follow through with this plan.

It was a chance to draw people to Luna Park for the owners, and also an opportunity for Edison to show how 'dangerous' Tesla's alternating current can be.

Using AC, Topsy the elephant was executed publicly executed on January 4th, 1903. There were over 1500 spectators, and over 100 photographers at the event. Video footage of the execution still exists today and can be found online!

The event was marketed as a 'first class execution' and was a huge news story at the time.

Topsy was about 35 years old at the time, which is about half the expected age that an elephant will live to in the wild.

Chapter 9:
Edison's Failures

For the most part, Edison is known as a success. He literally has changed the world, and the way we live today. His work will continue to be used for many years to come.

However, it wasn't always easy for Edison.

Like many success stories, he had to go through a multitude of failures throughout his career. His incredible persistence to push through these failures and keep on working is what really makes him special.

Edison's failures began back when he first started school. His teachers said that he was 'too stupid to learn anything', and subsequently, his mother home-schooled him.

As an employee, Edison could also be considered somewhat of a failure. He was regularly fired from jobs, including the first two positions he ever held.

Edison's real success came when he focused on being an inventor and entrepreneur full-time. But this is also where he experienced many failures. With good inventions, also come the not-so-good. The following is a list of some of Edison's inventions that didn't work so well.

The Automatic Vote Recorder

Edison had planned to save many hours spent counting votes by producing the world's first automatic vote counter. In theory, it sounded like quite a solid idea. This would allow people to vote on a bill, and have their votes tallied automatically, vastly improving efficiency.

But, in reality, it didn't go so well.

Edison took his idea to Washington where it was met with disapproval. Politicians feared that somehow tampering could occur, and that it would also negatively affect the voting process itself. His proposed invention was quickly dismissed.

The Electric Pen

The electric pen was somewhat of a success, and somewhat of a failure.

Edison initially designed an electric pen that instead of using ink, would punch tiny holes in the paper as it was used. This essentially created a stencil.

It was used on wax paper, to imprint a stencil on blank paper underneath, and was used primarily by railroad companies.

Edison mass-produced the pens in 1875. He sold them to registered agents for $20 a pen, and those agents then sold them to the end consumer for $30.

Edison eventually moved away from the idea after receiving a fair amount of negative feedback to the pens. They were too noisy, inefficient, and batteries had to be replaced regularly. They were also too heavy, and the batteries had to be maintained by using chemical solutions on a regular basis.

While it was a bit of a failure, the electric pen is said to be a predecessor to the electric tattoo guns used today!

The Talking Doll

In 1888 Edison created a miniature version of his phonograph, which he then installed into toy dolls.

Due to manufacturing issues however, they did not hit the market until 1890.

As soon as the dolls started selling however, they started to be returned. Customers complained that the dolls did not work properly, or broke too easily when used by kids. After a short period of time, the doll's voices would stop working properly and sound either faint or distorted.

Edison quickly took the dolls off the market and abandoned the idea, though it is the original inspiration for the multitude of talking doll toys available today!

Ore Mills & Separators

Edison wanted to become involved in the mining industry, and saw great potential. He looked to create a plant that could efficiently and effectively crush and separate rock.

To gain a competitive advantage over other in the industry, Edison made a large investment into building the largest plant of the time.

However, Edison had constant issues with the equipment, and plant design itself. He made modifications over a dozen times, but overall the project was a failure. This was a large project that Edison largely funded by himself, resulting in a considerable loss.

Uncharacteristically, Edison took an entire decade before finally throwing in the towel on this project, only making the loss even larger.

The Edison Home Service Club

In the 1900's, Edison designed and produced a range of machines that could be delivered to people's homes to provide entertainment. For the most part, these machines were designed to play music.

The business was called 'The Edison Home Service Club', and initially started in 1922.

Edison started by sending the paying subscribers 20 sample records per month that they could play. After 2 days, they selected the records they wanted to order, and sent the samples onward to the next subscriber.

The idea was sound, and worked well in some regional areas. The problem was, Edison didn't implement any mass marketing, or have the funds to do so. The project never took off nation wide.

It was a tough failure for Edison, but it taught him a lot about the power of marketing.

Failing 10,000 Times

Those are just a few of Edison's failures throughout his career. While most don't seem too bad at all, they could have been somewhat disastrous if they deterred him from trying again.

Edison is quoted as saying "I have not failed; I've just found 10,000 ways that won't work."

This attitude shows why Edison was such a success. He failed so many times in different areas, but each failure brought him closer to achieving his goals by simply showing him what not to do!

Chapter 10:
What Is Edison's Legacy

So, at the end of the day, what is Edison's legacy?

As discussed in the previous chapter, Edison experienced a number of failures throughout his life. Yet, we definitely don't consider him to be a failure.

Edison for the most part is known as an inventor and innovator. He definitely isn't most well known as 'elephant-executor', and in general we greatly respect Edison and his entire career.

Thomas Edison managed to change the world with his inventions, most notably, the light bulb. He has literally changed the way that we live and exist today, which is a truly incredible feat.

However, in my opinion it is not only Edison's incredible inventions that he will be remembered for. Mostly, I believe it will be his tenacity, and persistence to continue in spite of many failures.

That level of resilience is incredibly impressive and is something that every aspiring inventor or entrepreneur can definitely learn from!

Thomas Edison will forever be remembered as an incredible inventor, entrepreneur, genius, and inspiration for millions of people throughout the world.

Conclusion

Thanks again for taking the time to read this book!

You should now have a good understanding of Thomas Edison, and his incredible life and inventions! Hopefully this book has left you inspired by his amazing work and life!

If you enjoyed this book, please take the time to leave me a review on Amazon. I appreciate your honest feedback, and it really helps me to continue producing high quality books.